The Solo Squid:
How to Run a Happy One-Person Business

Susan Grossey

ISBN: 978-1-9160019-6-1

Susan's blogs:
www.ihatemoneylaundering.wordpress.com
www.susangrossey.wordpress.com/current-project-blog

Susan's websites:
www.thinkingaboutcrime.com
www.susangrossey.wordpress.com

Susan's other books:
    📖 "Money Laundering: A Training Strategy"
📖 "The Money Laundering Officer's Practical Handbook",
2006-2020
    📖 "Anti-Money Laundering: A Guide for the Non-
Executive Director" (five jurisdictional editions)
  📖 "Anti-Money Laundering: What You Need to Know"
(dozens of editions across sectors and jurisdictions)
  📖 "Suspicious Activity: The Adventures of an MLRO" –
parts 1-6 (e-books only)
📖 The Sam Plank series of historical financial crime novels,
set in London in the 1820s

DEDICATION

To Paul,
the best squid-wrangler in the land

CONTENTS

INTRODUCTION

This is not a book on how to set up a one-person business – on how to find funding or choose the right bank account or incorporate your business or register for VAT. There are plenty of books out there on these subjects, as well as small business websites and associations with forums for discussion which will give you the most current suggestions. In many ways, these concrete and practical decisions are the simplest part of running a one-person business: you can make a giant list of tasks and tick your way through it as you establish and run your one-person business.

And can I just be clear about this: I am talking about a genuinely *one-person* business. I don't mean a small partnership or a little company with four staff – I mean just you on your tod, your own-some lonesome. I don't care about what sort of business it is. Personally, I run an anti-money laundering consultancy. (In short, I advise businesses on how to avoid criminal money, and help them train their staff in how to spot money laundering and what to do about it.) You might be a gardener or a child-minder or a career consultant or a hairdresser or an independent financial adviser or a poet or an accountant – or anything at all, as long as you work alone.

Having your husband/wife/significant other step in with calming words, a quick hug and a soothing Jaffa Cake before you throw your laptop out of the window doesn't mean you don't work alone, but having a full-time business partner or colleague does. In the latter arrangement, there is always someone to share the decisions and the disasters, the concerns and the responsibilities, and that is an entirely different kettle of fish. The only kettle of fish I know is this one-person one, with just one large squid sitting in it, arms and tentacles waving madly trying to control everything at once, and if you too are a solo squid, then this is the book for you.

So if this is not a book on how to set up a one-person business, what is it? Well, it's a book on how to *enjoy* being a one-person business – on how to run a *happy* one-person business. Now I'm no fool: I don't expect to be dancing through the daffodils with bluebirds perched on my shoulders every day. I know that there are times when, frankly, it's all a bit overwhelming. But I also know that running a one-person business can be the source of the most amazing job satisfaction – after all, what is better than looking back at a project and knowing that you did it all yourself, from spotting the gap in the market to finding the client to doing the work to getting the money?

This book aims to help you derive the most satisfaction possible from your one-person business, so that even on the daffodil- and bluebird-free days, you can keep yourself going by remembering just how rewarding it is to run a personal business like yours.

SO WHAT DO I KNOW?

Recently I was watching a television documentary about midwives. Between all the screaming and swearing, one of the midwives said to the expectant mother that no, she hadn't had a baby herself, but she had studied and observed for many years. I'm sure that many people will disagree (among them, male midwives), but midwifery is one of those professions where I would really, really want personal experience to come into it. If someone is telling me "I know it hurts" and "it will all be over soon", I want them to be saying that from personal experience. So how do I know about running a happy one-person business?

I wish I could tell you that I was one of those brave and organised people who saw a niche in the market, saved up diligently, developed the business plan in my evenings and weekends, did some careful research, and then launched my new company with a fanfare. I wish I could, but it would be a lie.

In reality, I was working perfectly contentedly in the normal fashion – i.e. for someone else, with water coolers in every office, paid holidays and the glimmering promise of a numbered parking space – when I was made redundant. This was forever ago, in 1991, and the downsizing company got rid of four of us from my department on the same day. I sobbed down the phone to my boyfriend, who said something very wise: "I thought you said you were bored there anyway – why don't you go to the cinema this afternoon instead?" That redundancy signalled both the start of my addiction to going to the movies alone (you can watch whatever you like and you get all the Maltesers) and my forcible entry into the world of the one-person business.

Not that being a solo squid was my plan, not even then. No, I thought that I would get another job (you remember: water coolers, holidays, parking space). But while I applied to countless organisations, I needed to keep the money coming in. So I contacted a friend from university who had his own software company and told him that I had been made redundant but did he want someone to write his software manuals on a freelance basis? He did, and off I trotted. It turned out that he knew several other companies who needed a freelance writer, and by the time one of my countless applications had garnered me a job interview, you couldn't have forced me back into 'normal' employment at the tip of a red-hot and pointy poker.

I have been self-employed since 1991, although in 2003 I turned myself into a limited company – which I did only because I often work for large financial organisations, and many of them have a policy of accepting only limited companies as suppliers. Otherwise, I would have been quite content to continue as a self-employed individual. In other words, I have been living happily as a solo squid for more than a quarter of a century, and I have loved it. But is it for you? The questionnaire in the next section might help you decide, and – if the solo squid life is for you – the rest of this book aims to help you get the greatest happiness from being a solo squid.

IS THE SOLO SQUID LIFE FOR YOU?

I assume you are reading this book because you are considering running a one-person business. Much as I have loved my working life as a solo squid, I think it is important to recognise that it is not for everyone. Certainly everyone *can* work alone – but not everyone will *enjoy* it, and this book is about running a *happy* one-person business. So ask yourself a few questions:

* Am I content being alone for much for the day?

* Do I enjoy actually dealing with clients (their foibles, their uncertainties, their endless questions), as well as doing the work for them?

* Do I like the prospect of knowing more and more about one subject, rather than having a broader (but shallower) understanding of many subjects?

* Can I manage my own time, rather than needing someone else to organise my diary and plan my projects?

* If I am feeling low or poorly or bored, can I still push myself to get on with my work?

* Am I content to know, just for myself, that I am doing a good job, rather than needing external validation (in the form of pay rises, promotions, peer recognition, etc.)?

If you have answered yes to most of those questions, then you are probably solo squid material. (And cards on the table here: I cannot imagine a better working life than that of the solo squid.) If, on the other hand, you have looked at those questions and they fill you with despair, then running a one-person business is probably not going to make you happy.

Once again, this book is not about how to set up a one-person business, or about the practical administrative aspects of running a one-person business: it is about how to make sure that you get the most enjoyment possible from running your one-person business. So let's get on with that.

1 ENJOY YOUR OWN COMPANY

> "I paint self-portraits because I am so often alone, because I am the person I know best."
>
> *Frida Kahlo, Mexican artist (1907-1954)*

It sounds almost too obvious to say, but to be happy in a one-person business you have to enjoy your own company. Granted, your work will almost certainly involve seeing, speaking to and writing to people – unless you are a hermit-like poet who once a year sends a perfectly-crafted collection of verses, tied with ribbon and secured with sealing wax, to a grateful boutique publishing house. And even poets have to speak to the postman occasionally. But as the owner, managing director and big cheese of a one-person business, you will be spending a lot of time alone.

If you are lucky, you will have a supportive family and group of friends, and they will be willing to listen to your worries and pour you a stiff drink when it's all a bit scary. But even the closest friend or relative will baulk if you ask them to put together that last-minute proposal for you – the one you promised to deliver tomorrow – or enter those receipts into your bookkeeping spreadsheet, or wrestle with the printer's latest devious paper jam.

The buck stops with you

The long and the short of it is that running a one-person business means that the answer to every question beginning "Who is…" is "I am."

"Who is going to order new business cards for that conference?" "I am."

"Who is going to look into how much it will cost to accept credit card payments?" "I am."

"Who is going to tell the client that we can't meet the unrealistic deadline that they want to set?" "I am."

"Who is responsible for forgetting to call that client back as promised?" "I am."

I say all of this not to upset you – after all, this is a book about *enjoying* being a one-person business – but rather to show you that I understand it is not easy: having all the independence means having all the responsibility.

Those of your friends who are in more traditional employment will almost certainly have a ridiculously optimistic view of the life of the solo squid. They imagine that we roll out of bed just before nine, and have a leisurely breakfast in our jammies with one eye on incoming emails but most of our attention on daytime telly. They picture us doing a smidgeon of light work, perhaps going for a walk in a nearby park for inspiration, before breaking for elevenses, lunch and afternoon tea, and finally shutting up shop for a sun-downer in the garden at about five. I don't know about you but, apart from the jammies, absolutely none of that applies to me.

I've been in 'normal' employment for only a few years of my life, but I do remember that it was a doddle compared with running my own business – not least because at the end of the day you can leave it behind. And when you go off sick or on holiday, miracle of miracles! Someone else does your work! And you even get paid while they do it! As a one-person business, you carry your work with you wherever you go, like a snail. And when you do take time off, the work just sits there, waiting impatiently (and multiplying malevolently) for your return. But this does mean that no-one else sticks their oar in and mucks up something you have been crafting for weeks, or swoops in at the last minute to claim the credit for a project you've been masterminding for months.

I vant to be alone

So you will be spending a lot of time alone, and the cold truth is that some people can do this while retaining their chirpiness and sanity, and other people cannot. Some people fantasise about working alone, but if you actually take them away from the bustle of an office, from the constant interaction, from the buzziness and the chats around the kettle, they will seize up.

Others of us (I know this is me, and I assume it's you too, otherwise this is a strange book for you to be reading) actually prefer to work alone. I am an only child, so perhaps I was trained for solitude from an early age, from when I lined up teddies in my pretend school and bossed them around, knowing that they wouldn't answer back or complain to Human Resources. I always had my own bedroom and so was able to do my homework in a quiet, controlled environment, and when I put something down, it was still there hours later – not moved or eaten or destroyed by a meddling sibling.

None of this prepared me in any way for life in a shared office, with its constant noise and movement, and other people's inability to keep the place tidy. (I'm not saying that you have to be tidy to run a one-person business. If you prefer, you can give Snoopy's pal Pigpen a run for his money and keep your working environment in an advanced state of putrefaction, but the point is that it is your choice. So if you work alone, enjoy the fact that your 'office' can be in exactly the condition you want it to be.) And above all, life as an only child did not prepare me for that bugbear of modern working life: teamwork.

The joy of abandoning teamwork

It's akin to admitting that you throttle kittens as a hobby but I'm just going to say it: I hate teamwork. I know that it's extremely popular, that entire very large businesses are organised into teams, and that many offices proudly display sick-making posters with the motto "There is no I in team" and "Teamwork makes the dream work". But teamwork is most definitely not for me.

I am not saying that I cannot work with other people – of course I can. The key for me is the clear delineation of responsibilities. The client commissions me and tells me about their training needs. I then suggest some training that could suit them, and I design it. I send it to the client for review and they make some suggestions for improvement. I make the changes, and then deliver the training. It works well, because we both know who is responsible for what.

What would not work is if we sat down together and tried to design the training alongside each other. It would be slow and cumbersome, and often clients don't even know what they want (or don't want) until they see a draft form of it. And it would be disastrous if the client wanted to stand alongside me and share delivery of the training – once or twice I have tried this, at the client's request, and it's a mess.

When I go to my GP, I don't want her to say, "Goodness, that is an interesting set of symptoms – shall we look through this medical book together and see what we think is the closest match?". And when I go for a haircut, I don't suggest to my hairdresser that he does the back, which I can't see, while I have a go at the fringe myself. If I am stepping into someone's area of expertise, I am happy to let them do the work. And I expect my clients to let me guide them through my area of expertise.

It's not that I don't respect other people's ideas and suggestions, because I do. I simply don't find that teamwork is an efficient way to achieve things. I am more than happy to consult people before and after I do the work, but not during it. During it, I want to concentrate and work in my own way – and running a one-person business is ideal for people like me.

Create a professional network

Wanting to do most of your work alone and running screaming from any suggestion of teamwork does not mean that you should be isolated. Indeed, one of the main pleasures of running a one-person business is the opportunity it offers for you to create your own professional network of chosen individuals, rather than having to settle for the network foisted upon you by the company for which you work. As an employee, you may have little in common with your colleagues apart from working for the same company, and yet you are expected to spend huge amounts of time with them. As a one-person business you have no colleagues, and so you are free to build around you a group of people selected for their worth rather than for their proximity.

If all of that sounds a bit calculating, let me elaborate. In my own professional network (i.e. people I consider 'work friends' rather than 'personal friends'), I have:

* a banker who worked in compliance for forty years and has recently retired – I rely on him for the long view, to assure me that fads will pass and that common sense will prevail

* a headmistress with superb people-handling skills – she's the one I go to when I need guidance on taming an awkward client

❋ a regulator who knows everything, but everything, that goes on in a jurisdiction where I do a lot of work, and he keeps me up to date with any tasty developments

❋ a journalist who is brilliant at spotting (a) relevant news items, and (b) funny photos that I use to illustrate my training, and

❋ a lawyer who is always happy to check my understanding of a piece of legislation or my interpretation of a legal decision.

And – crucially – I hope that I am able to give something back to them. I am known as something of a Google whizz, and often work friends will ask if I can track down a story or a reference that they need – they know that I can do it much more quickly than they can, and for my part I am more than happy to help as I know one of the golden rules of the one-person business (of which much more in Chapter 6): give and ye shall receive.

There are many more formal networks, groups and associations out there that you can join, depending on what you are looking for from the experience. You might want to make professional connections with those in your field, you might want to make contact with potential clients, or you might want to talk about being a one-person business with others doing the same – and there is bound to be a group that will meet your needs.

I suggest going along to one or two events for a taster before signing up for proper membership or parting with any money. I once went along to a meeting of a local professional women's forum, imagining that it would be a place to discuss how to find a reliable accountant or whether it's worth having an office rather than working from home, but it turned out to be a big marketplace, with everyone trying to sell to everyone else. This might have worked for the colour consultants and flower designers who were in attendance, but anti-money laundering training is not something that your average professional woman will buy over a chicken salad sandwich.

Remember your life outside work

You may have noticed that I have been using two phrases almost interchangeably: *'running* a one-person business' and *'being* a one-person business'. When you work alone, and your whole working life depends on you, it can feel as though you and your business are one unit. In many ways this is a satisfying feeling – hence my wish to write this book and encourage more people to take the leap into working alone. But if you allow the 'one-person business you' to become the only you, other parts of your life will suffer – and so will you, one day.

(Of course there are times – as in any working life – when the demands of a particular project or deadline or client will require you to put everything else on the back burner for a certain period. But this should be the exception rather than the rule: no-one should be working like this, to the exclusion of all non-work, as the norm.)

Alongside the 'one-person business you', you need to make time for the family you and for the social you –

and plan time for both in your diary, otherwise they may well be shoved aside by work.

Family life

You may not want your family and friends to be practically involved with your one-person business. (Just in case you skipped the introduction, I should clarify that if you're actually in business with someone else – even if it is just your spouse or parent or BFF – you are not a *solo* squid and therefore this is not the book for you). However, I can say categorically that you will need their support.

You will need them to understand that sometimes your business has to come first – because if you don't meet that deadline or fix that computer or deliver those flyers, no-one else will. You will need them to take it on the chin if you are frazzled or distracted or grumpy (or all three at once – it happens). You might want them to listen to your problems and offer advice – my husband, with his corporate experience, is great at explaining to me how big companies (and their Byzantine supplier-approval processes, and their snail-like payment schedules) work. And you may need them to take up the financial slack if a client is late paying your invoice and you have a bad month as a result.

In other words, you could run a one-person business in the face of opposition from your nearest and dearest – it's your business and it's your decision – but probably not for long. In the final calculation, we all know that the one-person business you is less important than the family you, and it would be foolish to sacrifice the latter for the former.

Social life

As well as the support and understanding of family and friends, you will also need the balance that is provided by activities and interests outside of work – what I have classified roughly as your social life. It may be taking part in a sport or going out for a meal or to the cinema or travelling around the country taking photos of dry-stone walls – it really doesn't matter. What is important is that you are doing something other than work.

The benefits are manifold. You will be a more interesting, rounded person. You will make new friends, who will almost certainly have no interest in talking about your work life. You will get away from the office (or dining table or spare room or café corner) that you associate with work. And this will give your brain time to rest, regroup and recharge. This is essential for your mental health, and you will be surprised how often you will come back from a thrilling afternoon of photographing dry stone walls to find that you have suddenly thought of a solution to a business problem that has been vexing or paralysing you.

The key thing with your social life is to schedule it as determinedly as you schedule your work. If you leave it loose – "I'll see how it goes and maybe I'll pop out later for a quick swim" – it won't happen: work will always expand to fill the time. I'm not unrealistic – I know that sometimes it just won't be possible to get away – but do your very best. Put it in the diary and postpone it only if the work you are going to stay and do instead really cannot wait. In a one-person business there will always be work to be done – but is it work that has to be done *now*?

Top squid tips from this chapter:

🐙 Accept – and revel in – the responsibility that comes from being a solo squid

🐙 Create the network that you need around you – including other solo squids and professionals, and family and friends

🐙 Schedule your social life in your diary – and guard that time

Add your own squid tips for **enjoying your own company**:

THE SOLO SQUID

2 LOVE YOUR CLIENTS

> "One of the secrets of life is that all that is really worth the doing is what we do for others."
>
> *Lewis Carroll, English author (1832-1898)*

May I be blunt here? If you are a one-person business and you do not love your clients, you are setting yourself up for a whole shed-load of misery. I don't mean that you have to love them all, all the time – and I certainly don't mean it in any carnal sense. But I do mean that you have to get pleasure from thinking about what you can do to make their lives better and then from doing your best to do it.

The majority of my clients, for example, work in the compliance department of places like banks, accountancy practices, law firms, trust companies and so on. The law requires these people to put in place procedures to prevent money laundering, and my business exists to help them do that. With every client I meet, I am always asking myself what I can do to make their professional life easier. Can I rewrite their procedures for them, because they don't have time? Can I promise that all of their staff will receive the training required by law, because they don't have the time to deliver that training, or because they are scared of public speaking, or because their staff will pay attention only to an 'outside expert'? Can I make sure that everything is in place so that they can report to their next Board meeting that they have met their compliance obligations? And the key to it is that I get pleasure and satisfaction from doing this. If you are a problem-solver and a people-pleaser, the one-person business allows you to give full rein to these tendencies.

A quick aside: I call my clients 'clients' because that is the word used in the firms with which I work. You might call your clients 'customers' or 'patrons' or 'visitors' or 'buyers' or 'shoppers' – but it's all the same concept. We are providing a product or service and they are buying it. So when I say 'client', feel free to insert whatever term works for you at the time – good or bad.

Choose the clients you want

Despite my generally optimistic nature, I'm no Pollyanna (with her infuriating 'Glad Game'), and some clients can actually make me feel more like Eeyore ("Everybody crowds round so in this forest. There's no space. I never saw a more spreading lot of animals in my life, and in all the wrong places."). Indeed, I have one client whom I have vowed never to work with again because he was just so unpleasant – but only one over more than two decades is quite a good proportion, isn't it? And because I am a one-person business, I can make that decision for myself without having to justify it to anyone else or clear it with an exit committee, or – even worse – without having to stick with him because my employer considers him too valuable a client to abandon. He was horrid and demanding and ungrateful and I didn't enjoy working with him and I loathed speaking to him, and it's my choice. You can weather most storms with tricky clients when you know that you have that ultimate sanction in your back pocket: if they are just too gruesome, you can choose not to deal with them again.

Choosing your clients can be a positive action too. For instance, you can decide that you want to work only with clients who have the same moral outlook as you on things that matter to you. I know of a book reviewer, for instance, who refuses even to open any book that is not sent to her in recycled packaging. For my part, I once refused to work with someone who said, in essence, "we're only doing this training because the law says we have to – we're not interested in the messages and we certainly don't care whether staff really learn them". You can choose to work only with cheerful people or only with vegetarians or only with rugby fans – it's entirely up to you, and you will get extra satisfaction from knowing that you are living your work life in accordance with your personal priorities.

Charge those clients as you wish

You can also treat different clients differently, particularly when it comes to pricing. For centuries professional services firms have recognised the concept of *pro bono* work – where they do work for a reduced price or even for nothing, 'for the general good'. And now you can create your own version of this approach by adjusting your fee to suit the client – it's all within your control. My own fees vary according to whether the client is a commercial organisation, a governmental agency or a trade body, and although I make sure to increase my fees each year (more on that in Chapter 4), I sometimes offer clients the same fee as they paid the year before, if I think it's the right thing to do. And during the worldwide recession in 2007, I froze my rates for three years in sympathy with clients struggling in harsh economic conditions.

(I'm not naïve: I realise that when you are starting out as a one-person business you might well need to take on any work that comes your way, regardless of the client, and charge as much as you feel you can for that work. But as you become more successful – and that is surely the aim for us all – you will be able to pick and choose and adapt in a way that is never an option for the traditionally employed person, no matter how senior and successful they may become.)

Listen to how your client likes to talk

One of the most important lessons I learned early on is that clients are not one homogeneous mass – they are individuals. And one of the key ways in which they differ one from the other is how they like to communicate with you. Even in what might seem to be the most face-to-face of interactions, there will be communication options. My hairdresser, for instance, offers me the choice of booking appointments online or in person, and then to receive a reminder the day before by voicemail, email or text message.

In order to be most efficient and effective – and to get the most enjoyment from each interaction – you are going to have to work out the best way to communicate with each of your clients. And I mean the best for them, not the best for you: the aim is to use the method that they prefer, as this will make them most comfortable. You will learn quickly which clients are happier on the telephone, who will turn to email, and who prefers meetings in person. (Depending on your line of business, you may also have clients who contact you via text or social media, but this is not the case for me.)

Personally, I do not like conducting business on the telephone. Maybe it's my age or maybe it's my personality, but I prefer to deal with people either face-to-face or in writing. And as clients often want to discuss quite sensitive matters of in-house procedure (i.e. what their firm does to prevent money laundering) I don't want to do that in a public environment where someone might overhear. Moreover, the cautious side of me likes to get agreements in writing; when clients book my services I always send a confirmatory email outlining what we have agreed, in case of any future queries. But we live in the age of the telephone and it has to be used – and indeed you may well enjoy it tremendously and use it as an integral and welcome part of your sales technique.

Telephone tactics

The best piece of advice I was ever given on using the telephone was to smile before you answer. This makes you feel more positive and the difference shows in your voice – it sounds improbable, but I promise that it's true. The client may not know quite why, but they will get the impression that you are happy to hear from them, and that's always a nice thing to feel.

Sometimes a client will telephone me when I am in the middle of something else. It can be annoying and distracting and time-consuming. But I hope that the client never knows that, because an elegant and accomplished solicitor (an absolute expert at handling clients with diplomacy) once told me how to handle such situations. First, remember that smile. Second, if they ask whether now is a good time to talk, always say yes. (If what you are doing really cannot be interrupted, just don't answer the phone – why make someone else feel bad for your decision to answer their call?) And third, as soon as you can, ask them a very important question: "What can I do to help you?" It focuses their mind on why they are calling (so that they get to the point – some people can ramble a bit, which takes up your time as well as theirs), and it is always pleasant for them to hear that someone wants to help them.

And when you are calling a client, it is polite to ask: "Is now a good time to talk?" It is presumptuous to think that you can just butt into someone's working day and expect them to drop everything to concentrate on your matter. Tell them very briefly what the call is about, and let them decide whether they have the time and the information to deal with it now or whether they would rather talk later. (Of course, the situation is different if you are in dispute with them, for example over an unpaid invoice – I am talking here about regular client contact.)

Respect the client's confidentiality

One of your most important duties is to respect your client's confidentiality – both legally and in general terms. Do not tell anyone else that they are your client, unless they give their express permission. You might want to put their name on your website or ask them for a 'satisfied customer' quote or a reference, but you cannot do any of this without getting their permission.

You must always treat your client's information and data as carefully as you treat your own. If a client calls my mobile number and I am out in public, I will not answer and instead immediately text them to suggest that I call them back when I cannot be overheard; if they are hoping to discuss their firm's compliance arrangements, that is commercially sensitive information and I am certainly not going to be responsible for sharing it with a crowded carriage on the 1714 from King's Cross.

If you are a hairdresser or a therapist or a personal trainer or an independent financial adviser, you should not be telling anyone about who your clients are and which services they are using, no matter how beneficial sharing that information might be for your business (in the short term, that is – in the long term, clients will no longer trust you).

Stay friends

It depends on what your one-person business is, but you may have clients who go silent on you. In my line of work, I rarely work for the same client more than once a year, but I am lucky enough to have many clients who come back on an annual basis. And then some just fade away: they seemed perfectly happy with the work I did for them, but just did not come back.

Depending on how busy you are – in other words, how much you need the money – and on how much chutzpah you have, you could chase them down. Business wisdom reminds us that it costs more to acquire a new client than to retain an old one, so it may be worth your while to contact them and try to entice them to return (or find out, conclusively, why they have gone quiet). Personally, I have never done this: I figure that if people want to use my business they will, and if they don't, I don't want to embarrass them by asking them to explain, or get them back as a reluctant client. But I am scrupulous about keeping the door open and staying friends.

I never complain about a client to anyone else (except to my husband, of course, and he's not really listening most of the time). For many years now – it's coming up to its two-hundredth issue – I have offered a free monthly e-newsletter to my clients. (More about that in Chapter 6.) It's for clients only, but if someone stops being a client, I do not remove them from the mailing list. The fact that they were once a client is enough for me and anyway, it might not have been their decision to go quiet: if their corporate training budget is slashed, or if their boss is all in favour of computer-based training, or if their new CEO's son also offers anti-money laundering training, my client will have had no say in my fall from favour.

And it is important to remember that things can always change. My quiet client might move to a different firm, with a more generous training budget and a childless CEO, and there I am, back in the running – and this has happened to me several times, with clients re-emerging after a break of years. There are many downsides to falling out with clients, and none to staying friends. Plus, it's nicer – and being nice always makes life more enjoyable.

Top squid tips from this chapter:

Allow full rein to your people-pleasing tendencies

Think about your communication options, and work on your telephone technique

Stay friends with all your clients

Add your own squid tips for **loving your clients**:

3 KNOW YOUR SUBJECT

> "Sham Harga had run a successful eatery for many years by always smiling, never extending credit, and realising that most of his customers wanted meals properly balanced between the four food groups: sugar, starch, grease and burnt crunchy bits."
>
> *"Men at Arms" by Terry Pratchett (1948-2015)*

I assume that you are running – or thinking about launching – a one-person business because you have a particular skill that you think you can sell. You might make the most gorgeous jewellery out of seashells or give the clearest advice on structuring an investment portfolio, or know how to unknot the tensest shoulders or put those amazing stripes into people's lawns. Whatever your skill is, you must love it because – and this is controversial in these days of the gig economy and multi-part careers – I'm going to recommend that you vow to stick with it and become the go-to solo squid for that skill.

If you prefer lots of novelty in your working life, then it might make more sense for you to work for a larger organisation, where you can move between departments and take on different roles. If you want to work alone, that's hard to achieve in practical terms – there are no separate departments, and the only role available is solo squid.

I have met consultants in my area of operations who have tried, while working alone, to cover several bases: they offered training in anti-money laundering, data protection, bribery and corruption, sanctions and cybercrime. Although these subjects all come under the general heading of compliance, they are very different and – I would suggest – no one person can become an expert in all of them. Larger training firms could offer to meet all of these training needs, but only by using several members of staff. If you, as a solo squid, try to compete with their breadth of offering, you will come off worse. So I recommend that a one-person business offers not breadth, but depth.

Be the smartest kid in the room

When a client employs a solo squid, they are taking quite a chance. After all, there is only one person who can do the work for them – and if that person lets them down, there is no back-up. In order to make it worthwhile for a client to place their trust in a one-person business, they have to believe that they are getting something from that business that they cannot get elsewhere. It may be that you are significantly cheaper than the competition – although I hope not – but in most cases it is because the client believes that you are the best person for the job. And they will believe this because you can demonstrate how well you can do your work. In other words, when it comes to your subject, you are the smartest kid in the room.

When I first started out, I didn't intend to focus my whole career on anti-money laundering. (I didn't have the benefit of a book like this, so I had no plan at all.) I thought that I would do lots of compliance-related work, but – luckily for me, it turns out – I just didn't find the other parts of compliance interesting enough. Fraud? Nah. Data protection? You're joking. But money laundering? It is just the most fascinating subject, and it was love at first sight for me. I found every excuse I could not to diversify, even though everyone said it would be prudent to do so – what if anti-money laundering goes out of fashion (or out of the legislation), they said, or what if we solve the problem and money laundering goes away? They made many valid points, but by then I was in too deep – money laundering was the subject for me. The fortuitous result has been that, after more than two decades, I am a 'name' in anti-money laundering. I've been around for so long that people trust me to know my subject better than anyone else in the room. And that's what my clients pay for: my deep understanding of, and continued immersion in (some say obsession with), this one particular subject.

For my part, I get a great deal of satisfaction from knowing that I do have a high level of expertise – it pleases me to know that there is one thing that I can do better than (almost) anyone else.[1]   If, like me, you would rather do one thing really well than several to an average level, then you are a natural solo squid.

Some people are uncomfortable referring to themselves as experts – perhaps mindful of the old quip that an expert is someone who knows more and more about less and less until he knows everything about nothing, or perhaps simply out of awkward modesty. If you are self-conscious about calling yourself an expert (even though you are one), you might find the word 'specialist' more palatable. What you must not do is downplay your expertise because it is the very thing you are selling.

Enjoy your subject

It goes without saying that if you are going to devote your career to one subject or activity, it should be one that you enjoy. I suppose you could do some intense market research and then pick a business idea that seems to fill a gap in that market, but if you don't also love it, you have chosen a hard path.

In my spare time I write historical crime novels; they don't sell in huge numbers but I do love writing them. After looking at my unimpressive sales figures, a publisher advised me instead to 'write to the market' – to see what is selling and then write something in that genre. (Some of you may remember the humorous

---

[1] I came to this realisation – that my career preference is to be an 'expert' – through reading a book called "Career Anchors" by management guru Edgar Schein, which I recommend

writer Alan Coren; his agent told him that the bestselling books were about cats, golf and the Nazis – so he wrote one called "Golfing for Cats" and put a swastika on the cover.) Sound commercial advice, but the thought of spending a year of weekends writing something that doesn't interest me, even with the lure of large sales, fills me with gloom. Being a solo squid (and an author definitely falls into that category) is hard enough, without spending your time on something that does not make your heart sing.

Have fun with your subject

Unless your area of expertise is something that really cannot be treated with any levity at all (perhaps you are an embalmer), I can recommend introducing some fun into your working life. My training is about a serious subject (the money that flows from crime and the harm that money does), but I always try to include something light-hearted. It might simply be a story about a rather dim criminal (perhaps one who has put completely identifiable pictures of himself on social media, posing with guns, drugs and wads of cash) or it might be a quiz or game at the end of the training. There are plenty of game formats that you can use – the pub quiz, bingo, snakes and ladders – and if you source the questions from your subject, it's a way of learning or revising while having fun. And if you offer cheap, themed prizes, people like it even more – as I discuss in Chapter 7.

Master the shortcuts

Part of being an efficient solo squid (and efficiency leads to happiness, because it saves you time and money) is learning the shortcuts that can improve your working life.

One of my biggest shortcuts is doing repetitive tasks in bulk. Every month I send out an e-newsletter to clients (see Chapter 6 for details) and each time it contains a review of a book or (occasionally) a film. I do not write these reviews once a month: I spend a whole day in the library every six months and write six reviews at a time. This is more efficient because I am not interrupted or distracted partway through reading (as inevitably I would be if I were in my office) and because I get into the 'review-writing' groove. I do the same for my blog posts: I try to write three or four at a time and then schedule them for future publication.

Another shortcut is to re-use your material. Most of my training sessions have some common material – such as descriptions of the legislation – and I put this onto standard slides that I can download into every presentation. Of course I don't shout about this to my clients, as I want each of them to feel special and unique, but there is no point creating the same thing over and over again if you can copy it from last time. So box clever and get the maximum use from every piece of work that you do.

Top squid tips from this chapter:

Choose a line of work that you love and that makes your heart sing – and stick with it

Be proud of your expertise – and work to maintain it

Learn the shortcuts that serve you best

Add your own squid tips for **knowing your subject**:

THE SOLO SQUID

4 BE PREPARED

> "Give me six hours to chop down a tree and I will spend the first four sharpening the axe."
>
> *Abraham Lincoln, US president (1809-1865)*

When I speak to people who are not enjoying their life as a solo squid, what they usually say is that it's all too much for them, or that they can't keep up with the demands of clients, or that they never get time to enjoy their working life because as soon as one task is finished another three are waiting to be done. It is certainly true that running a one-person business can be very time-consuming and – as with all jobs – there will be periods of intense activity. But to be a *happy* solo squid you need to feel that (occasional emergencies aside) you are exactly as busy as you want to be, and that your workload is both stimulating and manageable. And to achieve this, there are a few ways in which careful planning at the outset – through creating systems and procedures – will save you both time and worry in the long term.

Keep tabs on your clients

It is vital to keep careful records of your interactions with clients, above and beyond the actual work that you do for them. We all have a 'contacts' system of some sort – perhaps within your email account or as a separate database or even in a retro Rolodex. For each client, note down their standard details – name, address, phone and email – and then augment that with anything else that is relevant.

For instance, if they mention that they are contacting you on someone else's recommendation, make a note of that. (And, incidentally, it would be polite to send a quick email of thanks to the person who made the recommendation, even if it comes to nothing.) If the client changes job, keep a note of their previous job. If they tell you something significant to them, note it down. I don't do it to be calculating or creepy, but if you're the supplier who can say to a client, "Welcome back – how was your daughter's wedding?", you're going to stand out as a real person in a sea of faceless competition. And it's far more rewarding in terms of happiness to feel that you are building relationships with clients and not just selling them things.

Be reliable

This is one of the most important pieces of advice I can offer. Remember that your clients, simply by using a solo squid, are taking a chance and placing a great deal of trust in you. They could take their business to a large firm, where there will be back-up if something goes wrong, but they have chosen you. And the very least you can do to repay their trust is to be completely and utterly reliable. This means sticking to what you say. You must supply what you say you will supply, by the date you promise and at the price you have agreed.

To make this work for you – in terms of time and profit – you must plan ahead and think carefully before you take on any commitments. It's easy, especially when you are first starting out as a solo squid, to agree to everything: of course you can take on another project, even though the deadline clashes with something else, and of course you can offer a discount, because the competition up the road always offers a discount. But if this means that you are going to be working through the night to complete a project at a loss, what is the point?

Occasionally – and you must make sure that it is only very occasionally – you will be happy to do this. It may be that the client is very important to you, and the squashed deadline is not their fault. It may be that the work is being done for a cause you support, and in essence you are giving your time and skills *pro bono*. Or it may be that you have let down this client before and you are now trying to make amends. But regularly doing work in a rush and/or for an unrealistic fee is not a sustainable – or indeed sensible or comfortable – way to be a solo squid.

Take control of your time

So you must be disciplined. In your diary – whether that is a traditional paper one or something more whizzy – allocate time for everything:

- ❊ appointments and meetings – both personal and business

- ❊ time required to complete work projects – block out hours, half-days, whole days or weeks

- ❊ time needed for business admin – such as issuing invoices, or working on your accounts (or dealing with your accountant)

- ❊ time to be spent on promotional activities

- ❊ time for recharging – such as your lunchtime walk around the park.

Come up with some sort of code – I use different coloured inks and draw lines across pages of my diary – so that you can see at a glance where the free blocks are and therefore whether you have time to take on another commitment. And review your diary regularly, to make sure that everything is in there and that nothing has changed that will affect other commitments.

I cannot stress this point enough: do not take on something you cannot manage. Clients are reasonable people, and if you explain clearly that you cannot meet that particular deadline but you can meet another one – and offer a realistic alternative – then they will understand (and will probably be impressed that you are in such calm control of your diary, which in turn will

assure them that you are indeed a safe pair of hands –
or octet of squid arms).

And if something goes wrong and you are not
going to be able to deliver as promised – perhaps you
are felled by a dose of flu or the client causes a delay by
not supplying what they agreed – you should face up to
this as soon as possible and let the client know. When
your own arrangements have been disrupted by being
let down by someone else, how often have you wailed,
"If only they had let me know sooner!". Don't be that
irritating person: let them know sooner.

Be boringly detailed

In the last section I suggested that one thing that
could derail a project is a client not supplying what they
agreed. This is why it is important for you to take
charge from the outset of agreeing with the client who
is to do what and by when. Let me give you the
example I know best, that of my own process for
designing and delivering anti-money laundering
training:

1. The client asks me if I can do some
   training.
2. We both consult our diaries and agree on a
   date for the training – in effect, our final
   deadline.
3. The client tells me what level of training
   they want – junior staff, compliance team,
   Board of directors – and how long I will
   have with each group.
4. I send the client a suggested agenda for
   each session – the topics I can cover in the
   time allowed – and alert them to any

contribution I will need from them (perhaps I will need to see their in-house compliance manual, to understand their procedures for taking on new clients), as well as telling them the deadline by which I will need their response (so that we can deliver the training on the agreed date).

5. The client agrees with the agenda, or makes changes to it.

6. I prepare the training material in accordance with the agreed agenda and send it to the client for their review – again telling them the deadline by which I will need their response.

7. The client approves the material or asks me to make changes to it.

8. I deliver the agreed training to the agreed audience/s on the agreed date.

If it sounds nit-picking, that's because it is. It is important, if you are to be *happy* as a one-person business, to be able to complete your work to a high standard without subjecting yourself to unpleasant amounts of stress.

Stress is an overused (and often misused) word these days. But I am married to an engineer and he has explained to me that stress is simply force divided by the area that can absorb it. Stress in and of itself is not negative, but it is true that a one-person business has less 'area' for absorbing stress than does a larger business (and so you will feel it more – you cannot spread the stress around). Obviously, systems are always designed to tolerate a certain amount of stress – otherwise your sofa would collapse the moment you sat on it. And in our working lives we can always stand some stress – indeed, some people (I'm not one of them but perhaps you are) work better if there is a bit of jeopardy in the set-up. But if you feel that a project would create too much stress – would cause some part of your system to collapse – then you should adjust the project. And one of the easiest (and most professional) ways to do this is to set the project parameters carefully: specify exactly what you will do, what the client will do, by which dates and for what price. And then stick to it (remember: the solo squid is always reliable).

Keep your pricing simple

One of the most mystifying and yet most crucial elements of working alone is knowing how to price what you are selling. If it is any comfort, most experts agree that pricing – especially for services – is more of an art than a science, and even big companies just make it up and then adjust it when the sales figures suggest that the price has been set too high or too low.

If you are selling something that many other people are also selling – haircuts, cups of coffee, annual tax returns – you can find out how much your competitors are charging and position yourself accordingly. But if your offering is significantly different from others out there, it is trickier. There are not many providers of anti-money laundering training, for instance, and I had to engage in torturous calculations to work out how many days of the year I would be training (as opposed to researching or writing), and how much money I needed to survive, and what fee I would need to charge to be taken seriously as a compliance professional, and then compare the result with other trainers in the financial services sector – it was ghastly. But I was keen to be able to present a very simple pricing structure to my clients, to make the decision easier for them, so I had to do the hard work behind the scenes.

And this is really the point I wanted to make: for your own sake and that of your clients, try to simplify your pricing as much as you can. Variations and uncertainties will cause confusion, which takes up time that you cannot afford to spend, and it may well also irritate your clients. So try, as far as you can, to be clear from the outset about how much your service or product will cost, and then stick to it.

For instance, I provide training. Many trainers charge per trainee, but I prefer to charge per day or half-day of training. In short, my clients buy my time and then use it as they wish. One client might spend a whole day on an in-depth, detailed training session just for their compliance team, while another might fit into their day four ninety-minute training sessions, each for fifty people, thereby training two hundred staff to an introductory level – but I will charge them both the same, because they have bought the same chunk of time. Many clients tell me how much they appreciate the certainty of knowing up front how much training budget they need to find, rather than having the final invoice vary according to how many people turned up on the day. It does not matter what you are selling: a simple and transparent pricing structure, which suggests that you are organised and reliable, will win you clients.

Another bonus of having a simple pricing structure is that it is simple to change. Few solo squids will have the time or budget to indulge in extensive market research or pricing analysis: you will simply decide on your price and see how it goes. However, once you have found your level, it is important to remember to increase it regularly to allow for inflation. If you do not, you will in effect be taking a cut in pay year on year. With a simple pricing structure, you can simply increase it by the rate of inflation – about 2.5% in recent years in the UK – each year, perhaps on your business birthday. It becomes an automatic thing that clients expect and respect, and saves you any agonising over or revisiting of your initial calculations.

Top squid tips from this chapter:

Design your systems and procedures early on

Agree everything, in detail – and then stick to it

Allocate time for everything in your diary

Simplify your pricing

Add your own squid tips for **being prepared**:

5 KNOW YOUR OWN MIND

> "I have heard your views. They do not harmonise with mine. The decision is taken unanimously."
>
> *Charles de Gaulle, French statesman (1890-1970)*

Life as a solo squid suits those of us who like to make our own decisions. When I speak to friends who work for large organisations and they tell me how every idea or innovation has to be taken to a phalanx of teams and focus groups and committees and considered from every angle before they can decide whether to use orange highlighter pens instead of yellow ones, I am grateful that the buck both starts and stops with me. And there are a few areas where the ability to make your own decisions without having to consider anyone else is particularly pleasant.

Defend your solo status

The one-person business is very common: many people realise that they want to run their own business (or, as happened in my case, they are made redundant from a normal job and can't find another one…) and they strike out on their own. But staying that way is a different matter. In our capitalist society, everything pushes towards endless growth. Look at the trend for chains and franchises; it's not enough to have one successful restaurant or gym or veterinary practice or bookkeeping business – you must replicate the formula and create more, more, more. Or do a search on Amazon for 'one person business', and you will see that all the suggested titles focus on how to grow from that one-person business into a million-dollar business or a global brand.

Almost since the day I set up as a solo squid, people have been asking when I am going to expand and take on staff and put together teams and tout for work in different jurisdictions. But I have friends who run small businesses – six staff, perhaps, across two offices – and they spend more time managing those people and dealing with admin than they do on whatever they set up their business to do. Taking on the responsibility of providing work for other people – even if they are only project-based freelancers and not full-time employees – is a real step-change. It's not for me, and so I have stayed resolutely solo.

That's not to say that my business does not grow – but it's growth on my own terms. I am always open to taking on new clients, as long as I am interested in the work they are offering, and as long as I have the capacity to do that work without placing myself under unpleasant stress (see Chapter 4). And every year I increase my rates by 2-3% (to reflect inflation) – you can be sure that your clients are increasing their prices, and if you don't keep step you will fall behind in real terms (i.e. in what you will be able to buy with your income).

There is nothing whatsoever wrong with staying a one-person business: it's not inevitably a stepping-stone to armies of staff, portfolios of premises and world domination. You have not failed if you stay solo. As long as you can make enough money to meet your needs (your current and projected outgoings, plus a little cushion of savings for lean times and emergencies) there is no obligation at all to trade in your solo status for that of an employer. Staying solo does not mean that you are not good enough or successful enough or imaginative enough to run a larger business: it simply means that you have chosen to run a happy one-person business.

Accept your squid-ness

Wonderful though it is, there is no denying that opting to be a solo squid will bring with it some limitations. No matter how determined and ambitious and innovative you may be, there will never be more than twenty-four hours in a day. And you will have to spend some of those hours sleeping and eating, even if you give up all other relaxation and activities entirely (which I really do not recommend). There is no point taking on so many commitments that you exhaust yourself (and risk letting down your clients with substandard or overdue work), so accept that – as a solo squid – you will not be able to do as much as a larger business, in terms of either range of work or number of clients.

Along with accepting your limitations, I also recommend that you resolve to stop feeling guilty about your solo squid status. No matter how successful you are, some people will always question your decision to go it alone. They will point out that you have no job security and poorer pension provision, and they will suggest that it would be more sensible for you to follow a more traditional career path – particularly if you have dependants who rely on your earnings. This may well be true, but it is also, frankly, none of their business, and you should not allow it to affect your choice to be a solo squid. Banish the guilt, which is a corrosive and useless emotion, and fill up the space it has left with more productive things like ambition and desire.

Stick to what pleases you

It sounds rather selfish when you put it like that, but one of the true joys of being a solo squid is that you can – for the most part – choose how you spend your time. I once knew a florist, for instance, who disliked doing wedding flowers. Actually, that's not quite true: she liked the flowers well enough, but she didn't like dealing with bridezillas and their mothers. So she took a decision not to offer a wedding service, and instead struck an informal deal with another local florist: if she received any wedding enquiries she would pass them on to him, and if he had funeral enquiries, he would return the favour. (Apparently grieving relatives are much less demanding and awkward than mothers of brides.)

Of course I'm not unrealistic about the working life of a solo squid; as I have said many times already, you'll be responsible for every aspect of your one-person business, including the bits you don't like. I loathe changing the toner cartridge on the printer, but it's that or blank pages. But those are incidental irritations: the majority of my working hours are spent on projects that I have chosen because I enjoy them, and not because they have been allocated to me by a manager, or dictated by the profit demands of a large organisation.

So you can feel free, as an established solo squid, to cast a critical eye over every piece of work that comes your way and say no to the ones you don't like, either because they're beyond your capability or capacity, or because they would bore or upset you. (I say 'established solo squid' because we all know that, at the beginning, you will take on just about anything – partly to pay the bills, partly to build a client base, and partly because you probably don't yet know which aspects of your work you simply don't want.)

Seek out other solo squids[2]

Just because you run a one-person business, it doesn't mean that you have to work alone all the time. You will have clients, of course, but you will also need occasionally to use the services of other businesses. For instance, I am a dab hand at doing my own

---

[2] I know what you're thinking: surely the plural of squid is squid. And so it is, if all the squid are of the same species. But if you are talking about several species – and I am – the plural is indeed squids.

bookkeeping but I loathe transforming all of those neat figures into my annual corporation tax return – and so I employ an accountant once a year to do that for me. And yes, he too is a solo squid. I like to give my business to other small businesses – and especially to other solo squids – and it's good to have an accountant who instinctively understands the nature of the one-person set-up.

Moreover, by employing another solo squid, you will know that you are getting the services of someone who – like you – is a master of their craft. I am responsible for every word written in this book but as for the beautiful cover, well, I have no artistic talent at all. Thankfully I know a solo squid cover designer whose entire working life is dedicated to creating gorgeous covers for writers (people who are adept with words but, for the most part, useless with images).

Top squid tips from this chapter:

🐙 Being a solo squid is a valid career option

🐙 Growth on your own terms – or no growth at all – is perfectly acceptable

🐙 Be wonderfully selfish in choosing your work

Add your own squid tips for **knowing your own mind**:

THE SOLO SQUID

6 GIVE AND YE SHALL RECEIVE

> "Be happy with what you have and are, be generous with both, and you won't have to hunt for happiness."
>
> *William Ewart Gladstone, British statesman (1809-1898)*

I wasn't sure where in the book to put this, as it is relevant to so much of my working life. I like to think of my professional life – well, my whole life, actually – as a being like one of those executive toys, where a nodding bird drinks and drinks and drinks from a glass until the weight of water makes him tip up and empty himself, and then he starts to nod and drink again.

Be generous

When I first started out as a solo squid, so many people were generous with their time, their advice, their expertise and their contacts. (Some weren't, but I choose not to dwell on them as they're not worth a single second more of my time.) The majority of people, when I asked them for help, gave it willingly – and often for longer and to far greater effect than I could ever have hoped. Now I am at the other end of my career, having drunk my fill like that plastic bird, and I take every opportunity I can to do the same for others who are starting out. Professional networks like LinkedIn and my own website make it simple for newbies to get in touch with me, and I always respond and always answer their questions as fulsomely and honestly as I can.

But this philosophy isn't just for the big, career-significant moments; I try to adhere to it at all times. I have always encouraged my clients to contact me whenever they want – even if we are not working together at the time. And they do: I get ad hoc questions along the lines of "Do you know where the Treasury has hidden that document they used to have on their website about arms embargoes?", or "Does a magistrate count as a 'senior member of the judiciary', for the purposes of assessing whether they are a politically exposed person?". Sometimes I will know the answer immediately and sometimes it will take me ten minutes or so to find out – but I am happy to help. That's partly because I love my clients and my subject (and am always happy to learn more about it), and partly because I know that one day I will have a question for one of them. How can I expect other people to take the time to answer my queries if I won't do the same? My area of operations is a small world: word soon gets around if you're awkward or ungenerous. And for my own sense of self-worth and job satisfaction, I'd rather be thought of as a guru than a grump.

Little added extras

Apart from answering ad hoc enquiries that people might send, I have two more formal routes through which I try to share information as generously as I can.

The first is my e-newsletter. Every client I have is asked whether they would like to receive my free monthly e-newsletter, which they can subscribe to simply by sending me an email. And every month about three hundred people receive a little digest of money laundering-related stories, pointing them to big cases, new legislation, thought-provoking reports and interesting research. Each e-newsletter ends with a review of a money laundering-themed book or film, and a silly financial crime story (this month, it's the woman who stole her employer's credit card and then spent large on glitzy costumes for her dog). I don't advertise the e-newsletter anywhere – it's simply a little something extra for clients, to show my gratitude for their business and their support.

And the second is my habit of firing off emails with appropriate links to specific clients. Whenever I am reading news websites or just tootling around the internet doing general research, I am on the look-out for anything that might be useful to someone else. I once read about some new initiative involving casinos in Malaysia, and I sent that link to three casino clients whose businesses have connections to Asia. And you know what? Clients do the same for me: most weeks I will receive two or three quick emails pointing me to stories I have missed. Businesses may be in competition, but I have found that individuals usually like to be co-operative.

Put your hand in your pocket

When I was at university I met two girls who shared a room. One came from a wealthy, privileged background and the other was the first in her working-class family to go to university. Whenever we went out together, the richer girl would wait for others to pay – probably because everyone she knew had money and it was a non-issue for her. But my poorer friend, despite her limited means, was always the first to throw her financial contribution into the pot, often insisting on paying for others. Being somewhere between the two (middle-class, middle income) I was so impressed by her generous impulses that I resolved to be more open-handed myself. Generosity is such an appealing characteristic, and so rare in the professional world, that you will be all the more memorable when you exhibit it.

If a client invites you to lunch, do not assume that they will pay; although they may well be able to charge it to expenses, no-one likes to be taken for granted. And if they do insist on paying, thank them fulsomely. If I am going into a consultancy meeting – perhaps delivering the results of a compliance audit to a board of directors – I will take a box of special biscuits. Yes, all big companies have catering budgets, but it is still a kind gesture (and even the most glacial finance director can be thawed at the prospect of an extra-chocolatey biscuit). It costs very little to make someone feel special and spoilt.

Remember your fellow solo squids

You shouldn't reserve your generosity only for your clients: other solo squids might also benefit from your time and expertise. From time to time someone who is thinking of setting up as a compliance consultant will contact me and ask for advice and I am happy to give it. Unless they are plotting to go into direct competition with me (and a couple of them have said that at the outset of what was a very short conversation), I cannot see the harm in giving them some help. Established authors often run writing masterclasses for amateurs, recognising that more good writing means more readers, which means more customers for all authors. Likewise, the more competent, reliable and cost-effective solo squids there are out there, the more people will come to see us as a real (and often preferable) alternative to larger businesses.

Be part of your community

Working alone does not mean that you should be isolated. In primary school I was taught how society evolved, from cavemen who were self-sufficient and then gathered into small groups so that they could share skills – the hunters caught the food while the builders tended the shelters and the fire. Then came the idea of a market, which meant that some people could give up hunting and growing and simply buy their food from other people, freeing up their time to sew clothes or dig for coal or fight battles. This specialisation increased and diversified, giving us today's society when very few of us would have a clue about how to catch our own dinner or build our own house. But this doesn't mean that we are no longer part of an inter-dependent community – and research shows that the happiest people are those who make an effort to connect with those around them. You may be a solo squid, but you don't want to be a lonely one, so take every opportunity to participate in relevant social initiatives.

Give something back

Modern businesses are encouraged to give as well as take – to have a social conscience and to devote a proportion of their profits to making improvements to the communities they serve. All of this is laudable and utterly correct, but as a solo squid it can be hard to know what to do. I frequently receive requests from young people looking for internships (what we used to call 'work experience'). And although I have plenty of work experience I could share, as a solo squid it would simply not be practical for me to take on an intern: for much of the day they would be able only to watch me doing my work, the majority of which cannot be safely passed over to a novice. There is no set of departments through which they can rotate to learn the business.

Instead, I have signed up to two programmes – one through my former university and the other through a professional network – which offer mentoring on a one-off or continuing basis. People new to work are shown profiles of those of us willing to share our expertise and provide a sounding board for them, and if they feel we could help we are put in touch and they can pick our brains.

Charity work and volunteering

Anyone who works in a normal office knows that a regular feature is the sponsored walk/ride/bake-off/whatever. As a solo squid you will not be asked to sponsor anyone – and conversely you will have no-one to ask to sponsor you if you decide to hike naked up Ben Nevis in aid of your favourite charity. But there are other ways you can contribute to charity as part of your working life.

I run several one-day workshops during the year – public events rather than in-house training – and at the end of each I ask people to fill in a feedback form (mainly to get their ideas on what topics I should include in the next workshop). To encourage them to participate, I promise that for every completed form I receive I will donate £1 to a specified charity. And each December I put a note on my website and in my e-newsletter to wish clients a happy festive season and to tell them that instead of buying and posting cards I am donating the equivalent amount of money to a specified charity. This is better for the planet (no paper waste), easier for me (writing and addressing those cards used to take two days), and a bonus for the charity.

As a solo squid, it is important to maintain other interests and activities outside work, which can otherwise become all-consuming (as discussed in Chapter 1). It can be easy to let good intentions slide in the face of workload and deadlines, so I ensure that I cannot do this by committing to regular voluntary work: I am a magistrate. (For readers outside the UK, magistrates – or justices of the peace – are lay people who sit in threes in court to hear less serious criminal cases, pass judgement and decide sentences.) Crucially, the magistrates' court rota is decided months in advance, so I cannot decide not to go just because I'm a bit busy – my work has to give way to the rota. And it is invariably good for my brain and my mood to spend a day thinking and talking about anything other than my work. Plus, of course, I am participating in the running of my community, which makes me feel good.

Be grateful

I don't want to sound like your mother, but one way in which the solo squid can stand out is by saying thank you.

It's a really easy way to keep clients happy and to stick in their minds, but it is often overlooked in more corporate environments. So if someone gives you their business, thank them – either in person, or with a short note or email afterwards. Don't use a hackneyed phrase like "we recognise that you have a choice of chiropractor/gardener/quantity surveyor and thank you for choosing us". Just say it from the heart: "It has been a pleasure working with you – thank you."

If someone gives you a contact or a recommendation or a link to a website or a suggestion for a new product, thank them.

If they email you to point out a spelling mistake on your menu or that your website is not working properly or that your flower arrangement died after only two days, thank them. It's invaluable to know when something is wrong, as it gives you the opportunity to put it right.

Thanking people with genuine gratitude costs nothing, it makes them feel good (and encourages them to deal with you again), and it makes your day happier.

Top squid tips from this chapter:

🐙 Be generous – with your time, money and expertise

🐙 Think about what little added extras you can give your clients

🐙 Give something back to your community

🐙 Always say thank you

Add your own squid tips for **giving and receiving**:

THE SOLO SQUID

7 BE YOUR OWN CHEERLEADER

> "I'm not the greatest; I'm the double greatest. Not only do I knock 'em out – I pick the round."
>
> *Muhammad Ali, American boxer (1942-2016)*

One of the hardest things I have found with being a solo squid is that you have to overcome shyness and modesty. I'm not saying that you have to go the full Muhammad Ali, but you do have to blow your own trumpet, even if you do use one of those trumpet mutes to keep the sound within acceptable levels. Yes: as well as all the other roles, you are also your own cheerleader – your own marketing and promotions department. On some days that will be an exciting prospect and on others it will seem exhausting. The kindest thing you can do for yourself is to timetable your cheerleading so that you don't feel guilty when you're not doing it, as you'll know that there is a plan.

First choose your trumpet

If you are of the selfie generation – comfortable with recording and sharing every haircut, holiday, meal and moment – this won't be as hard for you. But those of us who are older (and especially those of us who are older and English) find it remarkably difficult and uncomfortable to draw attention to our own achievements. As a solo squid you must make your peace with this and learn to toot your own trumpet from time to time, because no-one else will do it for you. If you are very lucky, clients will recommend you to others, which will bring you more business – but this is unreliable and unpredictable. For regular reminders to the world at large that you are here and that you are rather good at what you do, well, it's you on the trumpet again.

What you need to do is find the trumpet that you are most comfortable playing. Although I am not shy, I am not very good at networking for my own benefit. I'm good at connecting people with each other ("Elaine, this is Sally – you both grew up in Bristol and have horrid brothers"), and I'm a terrific matchmaker (I once introduced two friends whom I thought were single and would be perfect together, and it turned out that they were both already married – to each other!). But I am hopeless at the elevator pitch type of networking. I have tried to summarise my business into a pithy sentence ("I provide anti-money laundering training – I advise people on how to avoid criminal money") but I'm usually too busy asking questions to remember to deliver my own pitch. (I have always been terribly nosy about other people's work.)

On the other hand, there is nothing I like more than writing. So for me, my comfortable trumpet is the written word – and specifically, a weekly blog. I have been writing it for more than a decade now, and once a week I publish a few paragraphs on a hot money laundering concern of the day. I like to be a bit controversial where I can, and I don't worry about upsetting the police or the regulator or the government if I think they're making a hash of things. Over the years the blog has become widely read in my professional community and, coupled with my unusual name, serves as my calling card: the hope is that whenever anyone thinks that they need an anti-money laundering specialist, my name will come to mind.

Prod yourself in the back

If you are not excited about your own work, you cannot reasonably expect anyone else to be excited about it. Not every minute of every day is going to be thrilling – as a solo squid, you'll be doing a lot of tedious admin as well – but you do need to find a way to retain your enjoyment of work. This is essential both for you (otherwise work will become a chore) and for your clients (who will much prefer to work with someone optimistic and cheerful, and will choose accordingly).

In Chapter 8 I discuss the importance of taking care of yourself physically and mentally, in order to work most efficiently and effectively. But as well as general self-care, you need to discover what will motivate you when you're feeling – as you will on occasion – decidedly 'meh' about your work. In most working environments, you turn up on the 'meh' days because you have a contract to do so, or your boss will be angry, or you don't want to let down your colleagues – but as a solo squid you have to manufacture the 'oomph' yourself so that you know how to get yourself going again when you just don't fancy working. A day or two of being out of love with your solo squid-ness probably won't matter too much, but if you let that mood linger you will find yourself in a slump, and slumps are uncomfortable and miserable and unproductive. So on the days when you feel the 'meh' mood descending, you need to have your defences ready.

Defences against disillusion

Your self-starting prompt might be to remind yourself about the money you are making from the project – and not just the money, but specifically what you plan to do with that money. The most tedious piece of work can seem more appealing when you translate it into that exciting holiday you are saving towards (or that mortgage you are paying off, to keep the roof over your head).

Or you might remember how much your clients value you and your work. (In Chapter 11 I suggest keeping notes of the kind and complimentary things that people have said, which you can re-read to remind yourself that you do good work.) You might not feel much like doing yet another garden design for 'a small urban plot with minimum maintenance', for instance, but imagine how happy that client is going to be with their revamped outside space, and how much pleasure you get from sharing your love of gardens with other people.

For my own part, if I am feeling out of love with my work, I force myself to remember why I went into this business in the first place. I provide anti-money laundering advice and training because I think that money laundering is a dreadful crime that enables the vilest criminals to profit from disgusting activities like people trafficking and child pornography. And if I can use my particular communication and training skills to contribute to the fight against that, well, it's worth doing what I can – and my civic duty. If you can think back to the idealism with which you started your working life, it may well remind you how very worthwhile it is.

Do your own annual review

I don't mean those ghastly corporate things, with checklists and performance indicators and peer reviews – which, as a solo squid, you will be glad to leave behind. But I think it is important to schedule a regular point – and an annual interval works for me – at which you will look back over what you have done. The aim should be to analyse whether it is all going to plan and what, if anything, you can change to make your life as a solo squid even happier.

There are all sorts of things you might want to consider (perhaps using the other chapters of this book as a prompt), such as:

🐙 Do I have the right number of clients to meet my needs as a solo squid – or am I working too much, or earning too little?

🐙 Am I spending the right proportion of my time on the parts of my working life that energise me

– or have I allowed myself to become bogged down in the dreary bits?

✿ Does the thought of my work still put a spring in my step – or is it time to make a change?

✿ What are the three things I want to achieve next month/year?

I would suggest putting aside half a day for your review, and doing it somewhere other than your usual place of work. This will give you a literal and metaphorical change of scenery, and will also ensure that if your review throws up some tasks to be done, you are not derailed from the rest of the review process by launching into those tasks straight away. And don't think that this is one of those projects that you can slot in between other things. A review is hard to do piecemeal: it's far better to set aside the time and then work through the review from start to finish, leaving all implementation to another day.

Box clever with your marketing

As a solo squid, you will almost certainly have a smaller marketing budget than you would like. If you could afford to take out ads on primetime telly, fronted by George Clooney and Dame Judi Dench, you wouldn't need my tiddly marketing tips. But I assume that George and Judi are not on standby and that – like me – you have to find ways to be imaginative with a tiny marketing budget.

Marketing experts will disagree with me on this, I should imagine, but I don't think that a one-person business should worry about the more formal marketing techniques such as market research, client segmentation and targeted advertising. These are all excellent practices that can bring amazing results, but they cost a fortune and take ages – and solo squids have to spend their time and money very carefully. Rather, I recommend starting at the end and asking yourself this one question: what can I do to make sure that my clients remember me in a positive light?

I appreciate that this presupposes that you have at least some clients, but I think that is extremely likely. It also reflects the old marketing mantra that it costs much more to acquire a new client than to retain an old one. And so I urge you to concentrate on making sure that your current clients think of you often, and with fondness/admiration, and this will encourage them not only to return to you with further business but also to recommend you to others who will become your new clients. Much of how you can please your current clients has already been discussed in Chapter 2 (for me, it involves sharing information with them and offering them my e-newsletter), but there is still room for other activities that would come under the heading of marketing.

Souvenirs and novelties

Do not think for one minute that just because your clients are sensible, sober adults they do not like fun giveaways, because I can guarantee that they do. It is very much worth your while to do some research into good quality but inexpensive items that will somehow remind your clients of your business, and then work out the most effective way to distribute those items.

My line of work, as you must know by now, is the provision of anti-money laundering training. Whenever possible, I try to include a quiz or game in the training (to lighten the mood and as an excuse – via a fun format such as bingo or snakes and ladders – to recap the content of the training). And quizzes and games need prizes for the winners. I don't spend anything on customising the prizes – putting my company name on them – but instead choose quirky items on the theme of money. I have given out pencils made from shredded banknotes, and coasters of the locations on the Monopoly game board, and chocolate coins – none of them costs very much but they all bring a bit of silliness and a smile to the working day.

But although these little giveaways do not cost me much, I am very careful not to devalue them by handing them out willy-nilly: they have to be earned (by winning the quiz or game) and then they are treasured. My most revered and sought-after prize is a mug that I designed for money laundering reporting officers – the individuals responsible for overseeing their firm's anti-money laundering endeavours. These mugs are given out only at specific workshops and have become collector's items; one chap returned to work after a holiday to find that someone had broken his mug and he wrote me an impassioned letter pleading for a replacement. 'The mug' is always mentioned by old hands to new clients attending the workshop for the first time – and yet each mug (a simple white one with "MLRO" printed on the side) costs me the grand total of £6. Good promotional items do not need to be expensive – their value will come from the thought and imagination that you put into selecting and distributing them.

Cold, hard cash

I'm only kidding: I don't think you should ever give a client cash (unless you're running a bureau de change). But there are imaginative ways that you can save your clients money, which will endear you to them and perhaps also warm and amuse them enough to mention it to other people.

Special offers are always welcome and of course, being a solo squid, you can price your products and services however you want to price them. So if you want to offer a discount to mark your birthday or Bonfire Night or National Miniature Golf Day, you go right ahead. But in these days of online shopping and high street hysteria, straightforward discounts are not very memorable (and you'd have to offer 25% or more to catch anyone's eye). People will be more intrigued – and word will spread more quickly – if you can disguise the discount as something more engaging.

I once ran a 'shirt off my back' promotion in response to the entry into the anti-money laundering training market of two large consultancy firms. I emailed as many target individuals as I could find, saying that most consultants (hint: particularly the recently-arrived large consultancy firms) would take the shirt off your back, but that if they booked with me by the end of the month, I would send them a link to an online tailor for them to order their own shirt to the value of £50. So in contrast to the big firms, I would be putting the shirt *on* their back. They loved it. The £50 price of a shirt was significantly less than the discount I would have had to offer to have the same impact – and the beauty of it was that the reward went direct to the commissioning individual (i.e. the one who had power over choosing me) rather than simply being a discount that would be swallowed up, unnoticed, by their accounts department.

And you remember the workshops I mentioned? To thank people for attending regularly (I design and deliver a new workshop every year) I keep careful track of how many each person has attended. When they attend their fifth one, I give them a gift-card worth £25 for a chain of upmarket department stores, with strict instructions that the money is to be spent on a treat rather than on boring essentials. And when they attend their tenth workshop, they get a £50 gift-card. Again, this means that the person who is responsible for choosing the workshop actually gets the reward, and I know that most professionals are allowed to accept a gift of up to £50 in value without having to hand it over to their employer. Depending on your line of work, you can choose a gift-card that is relevant – perhaps a book or theatre token, or a voucher for a meal or a beauty treatment or a car-wash. The aim is to make your client feel that they are being a little bit spoilt because they are valued – and we all like to feel that.

Top squid tips from this chapter:

🐙 Find the trumpet that suits you

🐙 Work out how to invigorate the sad solo squid

🐙 Regularly check that you are still on track

🐙 Be personal and imaginative with your marketing

Add your own squid tips for **being your own cheerleader**:

THE SOLO SQUID

8 INVEST IN YOURSELF

> "We take better care of our smartphones than we do of ourselves – the phones are always recharged!"
>
> *Arianna Huffington, American author and businesswoman (1950-)*

There are two key aspects to investing in yourself: taking care of yourself, and taking care of your expertise.

Keep yourself healthy

We all know that prevention is better than cure, and for the one-person business this makes even better sense. If you are ill and cannot work, there will be no sick pay (unless you're catastrophically ill and have taken out the right insurance – but I'm talking about the usual coughs and colds, aches and pains). You may well lose money, because you can't charge a client for time spent moaning gently on the sofa and mainlining hot Ribena. And while you're out of action there is no-one else doing your work for you: it just waits for your return. So time off sick is all-round bad news for the one-person business.

Of course we're all unwell from time to time, but there are simple things you can do to maintain the best possible level of health, so that you're as primed as you can be to fight off illness. My top tips are these:

* Take time off to recharge – it can be tempting (and sometimes it's genuinely necessary) to work seven days a week, but make it the rare exception rather than the rule

* Have a proper lunch break – eating al desko is quick, certainly, but you won't enjoy your food, you'll get crumbs in your keyboard, and you need a change of scenery

* If your job is sedentary, stand up and stretch at least once an hour – and if you're standing anyway, move around to change position

* Go outside every day – looking into the distance will relax your eyes, swinging your arms as you walk will unclench your shoulders, and seeing greenery is known to improve mental wellbeing (from when we were cave-dwellers, and greenery signified food for us and our prey)

* Limit your snacks – my weakness is Jaffa Cakes, so I limit myself to three a day (I find that banning something entirely makes me obsess

about it, so I prefer to limit rather than eliminate)

❀ Drink a lot of water – dehydration will sneak up on you (it's the cause of most headaches) and getting up to go the loo after all that water will make you stretch and take a short break from your work.

Attend to your own mask before helping others with theirs

As a one-person business, what you are selling is your expertise. People pay you to do what you do because you do it better than they can in the time available. And whether that expertise is in cutting hair or building websites or completing VAT returns or tiling bathrooms, you need to keep your skills current in order to continue to provide your clients with the best service. You must offer value for money, and if your knowledge is no more current or in-depth than that of your clients, then you're not doing that. It will also give you confidence to know that you are working to the very highest standard.

It can be tempting to cruise. Time spent learning your craft is time when you are not earning, and it might even cost you money, if you have to pay for the training. But you should see it as an investment in your business and your future. My hairdresser tries to go on a course each year; it's not cheap, but he knows that he would quickly fall out of touch with hair trends and techniques if he did not update his skills. It is hard for me to find training that is specific enough to my needs – no-one offers courses in how to be a better anti-money laundering consultant – but I try to go to events or conferences that are relevant in some way, such as an update on financial legislation, or a demonstration of new training software. Podcasts are very popular now, and have the advantage of being flexible (you can listen to them whenever you want) and many are offered free of charge.

Maintain your enthusiasm

I have talked in Chapter 3 about knowing your subject and making sure that you are always the smartest kid in the room for that subject. This section is more about maintaining your excitement about it, and your joy at working as a solo squid in your chosen field (squids don't live in fields, but you get the idea).

My husband jokes that I can hear the phrase 'money laundering' at a hundred yards, and says that my ears almost visibly prick up if the subject appears on the news or in a book or programme or film – and he's right. Even after a quarter of a century, I am *still* excited when I hear 'my' subject being discussed – and it is that sense of excitement that reassures me that I am indeed working where I should be working. If your work bores you – even if it is secure and lucrative and important – you will find it a chore. I am not so naïve to think everyone can skip through every day of their working life with a song in their heart and a smile on their lips, but as a solo squid – with your added responsibility for being self-starting, and with no-one else to share the more tedious parts of the job – you need to choose something that, most of the time, makes you happy to be doing it.

One way to maintain your enthusiasm is to be alert to anything that could be relevant to your work. At the most basic level this means keeping your eyes and ears open for any news or developments that are relevant. If you're a hairdresser and there's a story in the news abut how plastics in shampoo are affecting the oceans, listen up: you could learn more about it and then become the 'ocean-friendly stylist' in your town. If you are introduced to a fellow solo squid at a party, pick their brains for ideas (most people love to share their expertise and recommendations) – and share yours with them in return. (It might be the start of a new professional network for you.) If you remain interested in and fascinated by your subject, your enthusiasm will be conveyed to your clients – and they will feel safe in the hands of someone who is always on the ball.

Top squid tips from this chapter:

🐙 Take time to recharge throughout the day and week

🐙 Regularly update and hone your skills

🐙 Maintain your excitement about your subject

Add your own squid tips for **investing in yourself**:

9 MAKE THE MOST OF YOUR FLEXIBILITY

> "It is not the strongest of the species that survives, nor the most intelligent, but the one most responsive to change."
>
> *Charles Darwin, English naturalist (1809-1882)*

One of the major benefits of life as a solo squid is that you can arrange your working life to suit you – and you can change it to suit you. Those who work for large companies know that even a small change can take months of negotiation and deliberation, whereas a solo squid can simply wake up one day and make wholesale changes to the way she works – and then change them back again the next day. Of course, anything that affects clients should be considered carefully – if you run a café, for instance, you shouldn't just change your opening hours without notice – but it gives solo squids a real business advantage to be able to trial new working practices and new initiatives without months of planning.

Relocate yourself

Some years ago we rebuilt our garage and put an office above it – this meant that I could move my computer out of our back bedroom and have a dedicated working space (which, crucially, I could leave behind at the end of the day). It is still my primary working space – and where I store my files – but because I don't have to consider anyone else, I can choose to work elsewhere.

When I am doing in-depth research involving lots of reading of learned books and journals, for instance, I will often locate myself in the local university library, because the hushed atmosphere of academic endeavour suits the mood of what I am doing (and they have lovely cheese scones in their tearoom). When I am trying to figure out something new – perhaps an agenda for a workshop, or a proposal for a potential client – I will sit in a trendy café in a student-y part of town, because the buzz and activity stimulates new thoughts. And I am writing this book with my laptop on my knee on the sofa in my lounge, as it is a personal project and I am trying to think about the effect that being a solo squid has had on my lifestyle and not just on my working life.

So if you're struggling to get going or make progress with a piece of work, a change of location might do the trick.

Do your sums

I talked in Chapter 7 about doing your own annual review. This will of course involve looking at your business – how is it doing, and what could it do better – but you should also take the opportunity to assess whether what you are doing is making you happy, and whether you could make any changes to increase that happiness.

One of my bugbears is that many people work to earn money without ever calculating how much money they actually need and want. Some years ago my husband and I sat down and worked out how much money we actually need to live comfortably. We want to stay in our home and have enough money to be able to take two holidays a year and not have to worry about making smallish but pleasurable purchases (a new pair of shoes, a dinner out followed by the cinema). We also want to have a reasonable cushion of savings in case the washing machine dies or we need to buy an emergency plane ticket to see a sick friend, and be able to put money aside in a pension scheme. But we don't care about buying new cars, and neither of us smokes or is in the grip of an expensive hobby.

So we did our sums (it only took about an hour), added 15% for good measure, and came up with how much we need to bring in each year to achieve a standard of living that meets our definition of 'comfortable'. From looking back at my business accounts I knew that I could reach my half of the target as a solo squid, and each year I check that this is still the case. And if I do go through a dry spell with work, I can retain a sense of perspective – and keep the panic at bay – by making sure that, overall, I am still going to meet my target.

We all know people who work and work and work, to the exclusion of all else, and I often wonder whether they know what they are aiming for – apart from 'more'. I have found it much healthier – and much more satisfying – to think instead of 'enough'. I calculate what is 'enough' for me and I work towards that. If you don't set a target, how will you know when you have reached it? There are few feelings as wonderful as reaching a goal, and as a solo squid you have the marvellous liberty of setting your own goals, rather than having to work towards goals set by someone else, with which you might not even agree. So each year – or at whatever interval suits you – check that you are still happy with your goals and targets.

Stay true to yourself

'Change' is a big theme in business, as is 'growth'. (Remember that I talked in Chapter 5 about having the courage to stay solo.) And of course, if something is not working as you had hoped, or if some part of your life as a solo squid is making you unhappy, then you should change it.

But equally, if you like how something is working and it suits you, then you should not feel obliged to update or otherwise change it. For instance, I have a company website. I created it myself – of course – about fifteen years ago. And although I update it every day (I have a Newsroom page where I put links to money laundering stories in the media), the look and structure of the website has not changed. Nowadays it seems very old-fashioned – it's what web designers sneeringly call a 'shopfront site', with no clever scrolling, 'Buy Now' facility or embedded content. And every few months a web designer will contact me out of the blue and offer to update the site – but there is no need. The website does what I want: it explains who I am and what I do and where to find me. It is not intended to lure in new clients, as all my work – all of it – comes through word of mouth, and potential clients go to the website simply to check that I sound reputable. My old-fashioned website works for me: it gives people the information they need, and it is simple enough for me to maintain.

When Twitter was first gaining traction, I set up a Twitter handle for my business and religiously tweeted several times a day, circulating money laundering stories that I found. But when I asked clients whether they found it useful, they said they never looked at it: in the (rather conservative) financial sector which is home to most of my clients, it is frowned upon to look at Twitter at work. It was taking me about thirty minutes a day to source and share the stories which no-one was seeing, so I stopped using Twitter for work – even though every marketing person on the planet will tell you that it is an essential business tool. No-one knows better than you what works for your business and your clients, so don't be afraid to swim against the tide and stick with the bits that are worth your time.

Top squid tips from this chapter:

🐙 Change the view

🐙 Work out what is 'enough' for you

🐙 If it suits you, stick with it regardless of fashion

Add your own squid tips for **making the most of your flexibility**:

10 DON'T TAKE IT TOO SERIOUSLY

> "Never be afraid to laugh at yourself; after all, you could be missing out on the joke of the century."
>
> *Dame Edna Everage, Australian housewife and megastar*
> *(1934-)*

One of the dangers of being a solo squid is that your business can take over your life: because it is all down to you, you start to think that it is all that matters. Of course it is important that you make enough money to meet your commitments, while using your skills to the best of your ability – but your working life is only one part of you.

Keep your distance

In Chapter 1 I encouraged you to develop and maintain your interests outside work so that you have a more rounded and varied life. A bit of distance will allow perspective on your business. You will then have a more objective view of things, which will help you to see where change is needed – and which will be invaluable if things go wrong. If you do hit a stumbling block – you lose an important client, or you are ill and cannot work for a while, or the law changes and you have to adapt your business – you will cope much better if you can see your work as only a part of your life rather than as your entire identity. And there are other benefits to reminding yourself that you are not simply a solo squid – you are also a spouse or a parent or a special constable or a cyclist or a gardener.

Laugh at your mistakes

We all get it wrong sometimes. I once sent out my e-newsletter to about forty people without hiding their email addresses from each other. Last month I missed the deadline for filing my VAT return. And early in my training career, I clumsily fell off a stage in front of four hundred people, thereby revealing my undies to them all. Each mistake was annoying in its own way, but none was worth dwelling on or berating myself about. I apologised for them all (after all, they were all my mistakes – there is no-one else for the solo squid to blame) and resolved to do better in future. I can't say that I laughed about the VAT mistake, as it took ages to sort out, but it was far from catastrophic. I altered my email settings so that I can't make that mistake again with the e-newsletter. And as for the flashing, well, we all laughed at that one.

In short, it's important to be gentle on yourself. You wouldn't be angry with a friend for making an honest mistake, so why be angry with yourself?

Apologise if anyone else is involved, work out what went wrong and how to stop it happening again, and then have an extra chocolate biscuit to show that you have forgiven yourself.

Accept that you can't do everything

You are a solo squid, not a superman/woman. You cannot do everything. The myth about 'having it all' that has tormented working parents for decades applies equally to those who work alone. Life is a series of compromises and choices – time can be spent only once, and if you spend it on activity one it is no longer available for activity two.

By definition, solo squids undertake to do everything in their business, but – as I discussed in Chapter 5 – you will almost certainly want to buy in other skills (an accountant, or a website designer, or a cake decorator). This makes perfect sense: why spend hours researching insurance companies and their offerings when a specialist insurance adviser can point you to the right policy in minutes? Do the simple maths: if you can earn more in the time you save than you will spend on employing the expert, then do it – you're saving money.

Even if it won't save you money, will it save you irritation or unhappiness? Will it free you up to do something – perhaps even something not related to your business – that you find more energising and enjoyable? Again, be gentle on yourself: you are not a failure as a solo squid if you ask others for help.

Top squid tips from this chapter:

🐙   Get some perspective on your business

🐙   Admit your mistakes and move on

🐙   Spend your time wisely

Add your own squid tips for **not taking it too seriously**:

11 DO TAKE THE CREDIT

> "When you cannot get a compliment any other way, pay yourself one. I can live two months on a good compliment."
>
> *Mark Twain, American author (1835-1910)*

Although we solo squids may shed few tears at the prospect of missing out on annual appraisals and performance reviews, the downside is that there is no-one else to give you a high five and a jam doughnut when you have done well. As with all things squid, the only one who can do this is you – so you must make sure you do it.

Keep a record of the good times

When you work alone and all your income has to come from your own endeavours, it can be tempting simply to ignore the triumphs and just to carry on with the next project on the list. This is a mistake: you must pause and enjoy the moment.

Early in my career as a solo squid I started a little tradition: every time a project went particularly well – if a client emailed me after a day of training to say how pleased they were, or if my workshop feedback was uniformly positive – I allowed myself an hour and £20 in my local bookshop, to choose and buy a hardback book. These books – unrelated by topic or genre or author – have their own shelf in my house and are a reminder that I have done good work.

If you don't want to mark a triumph with a purchase, you could allow yourself an afternoon off work, or a telephone call to a friend, or something else that reminds you that you have done well.

And if the positive feedback comes in the form of an email or – rare these days – a written letter, make sure to keep a copy in a separate folder. There will be down days, when work is not going well and perhaps you fear that being a solo squid is a terrible mistake and you'll never find another client – and on those days, a glance through the evidence to the contrary will lift your mood and encourage you to stick with it.

Enjoy the compliments

When someone offers a compliment – whether it is about your hair or your cooking or your work – you might well downplay it. "It's not as good as the one you made us last time", you might say of the meal they praise – which sadly makes you both feel worse. If a client offers you a compliment, accept it with grace, acknowledging the effort that went into the work, and then find a more productive way to compliment them in return. If one of my clients says that a training session has gone well and that their staff enjoyed it, I will reply, "Yes, I felt that too – the effort we put into designing the content has certainly paid off." And in this way I agree that the work is praiseworthy, and I also point out their part in its success – a double win, making both of us feel better.

And remember too that people can compliment you in unspoken ways. For most businesses, the greatest and most sincere of compliments is repeat business. If a client is pleased enough with my work to pay for it all over again, I know that I have done a good job. So every time a client comes back, take that for the enormous compliment that it is – and bask in the moment.

Stand up for your value

I do not want to stray here into giving practical business advice, but one important way to take credit for the work you do is to be firm about prompt and fair payment for that work. Price your work realistically – as discussed in Chapter 4. Make sure that your invoices state your payment terms (as agreed with the client before you took on the work), and chase clients relentlessly – through the courts if necessary – if they overstep those terms. If you take your value seriously, so will your clients.

Celebrate good times, come on!

On a happier note, your working life should include regular celebrations. If you get a particularly noteworthy piece of work, mark it in some way.

(Whenever I publish one of my historical novels, I buy myself a small piece of jewellery from the Regency period – which is the setting of the books.)

Try to remember the date on which you set up your business so that you can celebrate its birthday. I have a certificate of incorporation noting the day on which I created my limited company, and every year I take myself out for lunch on that day (and also use it as the date on which I increase my fees, as recommended in Chapter 5). On my fifth corporate birthday I sent chocolate coins to all my clients, and on my tenth – by which point I had too many clients for that – I emailed them all to thank them for their custom and support, and made a donation to a charity instead.

One of the highlights of the year for people working as employees is the Christmas party (or similar celebration for other religions). As a solo squid you certainly do not have to miss out. Contact a handful of other solo squids in your neighbourhood and arrange a shared party with them – perhaps a lunch in a local pub, or a visit to an ice-rink or pantomime. Alternatively, find out if you have a local care home or hospice that would appreciate help with its own Christmas meal or outing. As a solo squid you can choose exactly the celebration that you will most enjoy and that will most fittingly mark the occasion, rather than having to go along with what others have planned.

Top squid tips from this chapter:

🐙 Wallow in the compliments – and particularly in repeat business

🐙 Be professional about being paid

🐙 Celebrate your corporate milestones

Add your own squid tips for **taking the credit**:

THE SOLO SQUID

12 KNOW WHEN TO SAY GOODBYE

> "I have no intention of uttering my last words on the stage. Room service and a couple of depraved young women will do me quite nicely for an exit."
>
> *Peter O'Toole, British actor (1932-2013)*

Nothing is forever – not even being a solo squid. Your circumstances may change, requiring you to stop work for a while, or to take a part-time job, or to move abroad. Your market may change, altering the viability of your current business. Or you may just fall out of love with being a solo squid and decide that you want to retire or let someone else take all the responsibility (also known as 'being an employee'), or do the coastal path on roller-skates. All of this is absolutely fine – you just need to find the right way to say goodbye.

You will want to leave on a positive note, I am sure. If you have clients who might miss you, be sure to let them know when (and why) you will be shutting up shop. If you can, suggest an alternative business they can use instead of yours – but only if it is a genuine recommendation. You don't want them cursing you later if they try the new place and it's dreadful.

If yours is the sort of business with assets that can be sold (including intellectual property and patents as well as physical assets), start thinking about this well in advance – you certainly don't want to be offloading things in a fire sale, as you will regret every penny you lose. You might well need to take professional advice about business exits and future tax considerations, particularly if yours is a limited company or if you have a company pension.

If you can, choose an end date that suits you. The idea of closing at the end of a calendar year or your company accounting year might appeal to your sense of completion, or you might want to bow out on a significant birthday, or in time for a big life event such as a fabulous holiday or a family gathering.

You can expect to experience jitters as you work towards the exit. You may wonder whether you are doing the right thing, and you may – understandably – remember only the good things about being a solo squid while conveniently forgetting the irritations. But as long as you are finishing for the right reasons (and for your own reasons – not someone else's), you will be fine.

That said, if you change your mind and decide that you want to carry on as a solo squid, then that's fine too. Remember, the joy of working alone is that you don't have to justify your decisions to anyone except yourself, and nor do you have to take the feelings or plans of colleagues or employees into account.

And before you do finally leave, take some time to reflect on everything you have achieved as a solo squid. Look back through that scrapbook of lovely comments. Review your client list and remember the projects you have worked on with them. Look around you at the business you have created, which has fed you and clothed you and housed you and paid the bills and bought you holidays and meals and treats. And congratulate yourself for it all – you are indeed a solo squid.

Top squid tips from this chapter:

🐙 Remember that nothing is forever – not even being a solo squid

🐙 Try to help clients to find an alternative provider

🐙 Congratulate yourself for living life as a solo squid

Add your own squid tips for **knowing when to say goodbye**:

ABOUT THE AUTHOR

Susan has worked in the anti-money laundering field for over twenty-five years, initially for large companies and then for a specialist partnership. In 2003 she set up Thinking about Crime Limited, a dedicated anti-money laundering consultancy of just herself.

In her idle moments, she writes historical financial crime fiction.

If you have any questions, please email Susan:
susan@thinkingaboutcrime.com

If you have enjoyed this book, why not relax after work with one of Susan's novels, all dealing with financial crime in London in the 1820s

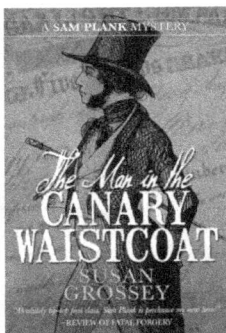

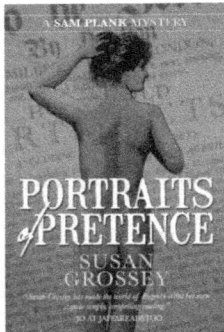

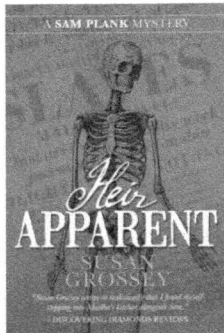